Collins Primary Sc

# FORCES AND ENERGY

Linda Howe

# Acknowledgements


ISBN 0 00 317582 0
Published by Collins Educational an imprint of
HarperCollins *Publishers,* London and Glasgow

Design by Shireen Nathoo
Illustrations by Helen Herbert (Graham-Cameron
Illustration), Sally Neave, Gay Galsworthy,
Cover illustration by Debi Ani
Commissioned photography by Oliver Hatch

Typeset by Kalligraphic Design Ltd., Horley, Surrey
Printed and bound in Hong Kong



The publishers thank Beyton Middle School, Suffolk
and Fielding Middle School, London for their
kind co-operation in the production of
Collins Primary Science.

Photographs - The publishers would like to thank the
following for permission to reproduce photographs:

Barnabys Picture Library 12(tl), 38(t), 40(t), 42(t);
The J Allan Cash Photolibrary 1(tr), 12(tr), 14 (t,c), 23
(cl,cr,cc), 30; Robert Harding Picture Library 1 (tl, bl, br),
12(br,bl), 19(t); Frank Lane 31(t)

t = top, b = bottom, c = centre, l = left, r = right

# Contents

# HELPFUL NOTES

In these books you will be:

- ★ trying out ideas
- ★ seeing what you can find out
- ★ making and using models
- ★ using different ways to show what you find out

Look out for these signs and they will help you.

This sign is at the beginning of each activity.
The activities give you ideas for things you can make, things you can try and ways of finding things out.

This sign tells you what you need to collect before you begin an activity. Things that you might need are shown in the box. If you can't find all the things in the list think of other things in your classroom that you could use instead. Remember that we just give you ideas for materials to use. You may need to find other things so that you can try out your own ideas.

This sign asks you to think of ideas of your own.
Always talk your ideas over with a friend as they can usually help you with your thinking.
Before you try a test of your own, plan it carefully.
Remember these things:

1. Think about what you want to make, try, or find out.
2. Collect what you need.
3. Try out your ideas. Can you improve them in any way?
4. Record what you have done.

It is important to work safely and carefully. Sometimes, when you are using tools or handling hot things, you will need to take special care. This sign tells you when to take extra care.

**FIND OUT**

When you see this sign you will need to find things out for yourself. You will need to decide how to find out what you need. You may need to:

- look in some books from the library
- write some letters
- ask other people
- look closely at some pictures, the television or a video.

**RECORD**

When you are doing an activity you will need to think about how you will show what you find out. Sometimes you will need to choose a way that will help you remember what you have done and sometimes you will need to choose a way that will tell other people what you have found out. There are lots of ways of recording your activities. Here are some for you to choose from:

- making a chart or table
- writing a list
- drawing a picture
- taking a photograph
- keeping notes while you are working
- making a tape recording
- using a computer fact file
- writing about what you have done

# 1 BUILDING FOR STRENGTH

Castles were built in the Middle Ages to keep people safe from their enemies. They had to be strong to stay standing when they were attacked.
Look at these photographs of different castles.
For each castle, think about:

- where it was built
- what materials were used
- what shapes were used
- how else it was made strong.

Chepstow Castle

Harlech Castle

Deal Castle

Bodiam Castle

## ACTIVITY

Look at these photographs of different castles. Draw and complete this table for each castle.

| Name of castle | materials used | shape used | strengthened by |
|---|---|---|---|
| 1 | | | |
| 2 | | | |
| 3 | | | |
| 4 | | | |

# Strength and shape

Card • weights • your own ideas

**ACTIVITY**

When people build things today they still have to use strong shapes. Plan a fair test to find out which shapes are strongest? You could:

- use card towers and weights
- make some tunnel shapes
- or use your own ideas.

Plan how you will do your test. Write down how you will make it a fair test before you start:

- will you make each shape from the same material?
- will you test each shape in the same way?
- will you need to time or take measurements?

Carry out your test.

**RECORD**

Record your results like this. Which shapes would you use for a strong building?

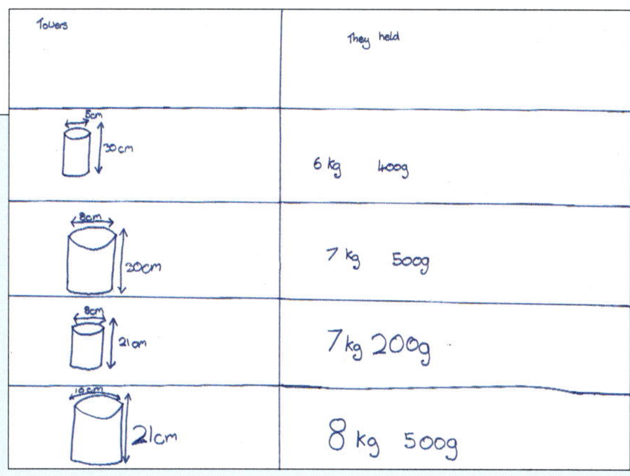

| Towers | They held |
|---|---|
| 5cm, 30cm | 6 kg 400g |
| 8cm, 20cm | 7 kg 500g |
| 8cm, 21cm | 7 kg 200g |
| 10cm, 21cm | 8 kg 500g |

# 2 BUILDING BRICKS

## ACTIVITY – A –

The oldest building bricks were made by baking clay shapes in the sun. Can you use this 'recipe' to make some bricks like the ones Egyptians used thousands of years ago? Plan an investigation to find out if the bricks would have been stronger with or without the straw?

Think about how you will test and what you will need. Talk to your teacher about your plan.

Carry out your investigation.

Write down what you did and what you found out.

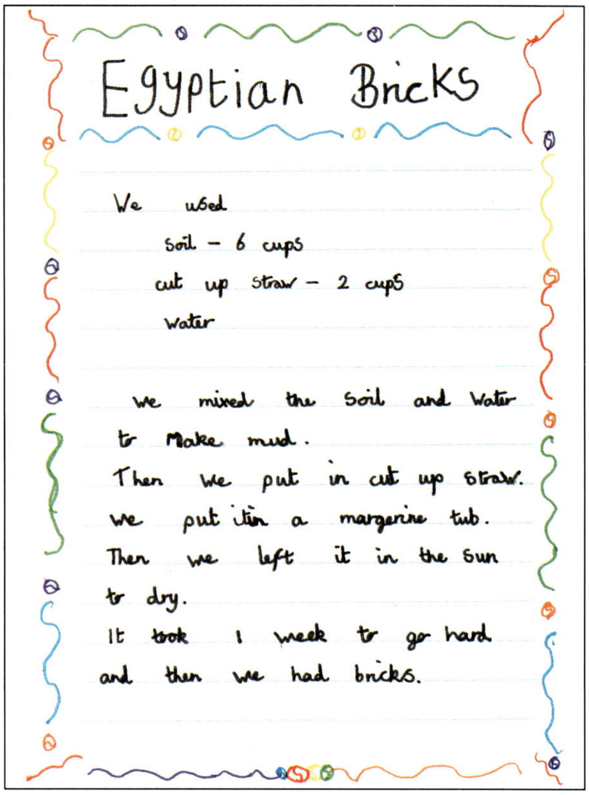

Egyptian Bricks

We used
soil – 6 cups
cut up straw – 2 cups
water

we mixed the soil and water to make mud.
Then we put in cut up straw.
we put it in a margarine tub.
Then we left it in the sun to dry.
It took 1 week to go hard and then we had bricks.

## ACTIVITY – B –

Modern bricks are still made from a clay mixture. They are *fired* in a very hot oven. Look at these bricks. Make a list of things which are the same and things which are different about them.

Different bricks are used for different things. They can be waterproof, or strong and heavy, or they can be lightweight but damaged by cold. Which bricks would you use for:

- an inside wall?
- a cellar wall under the ground?
- a brick barn?

# Which is the strongest pattern?

Wooden building blocks or other "bricks" • your own ideas for testing

Walls can be built using different patterns of bricks.
The main kinds of pattern are:

English Stretcher Flemish Open

Plan a test to find out which pattern makes the strongest wall.

Think about:

- how you will test
- how you will make your test fair
- how you will show your results.

Can you use your results to choose which pattern of bricks you would use to build:

- a tall building?
- a small garden wall?

# 3 MIXING CONCRETE

Concrete is a strong material used for making paths, buildings and bridges. It is made by mixing *cement*, sand, stones and water.

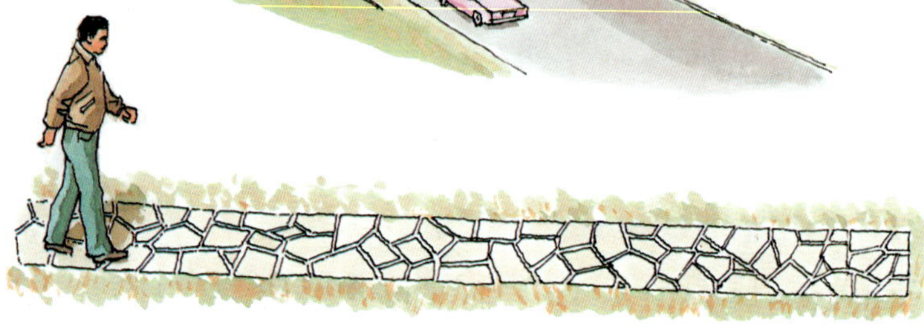

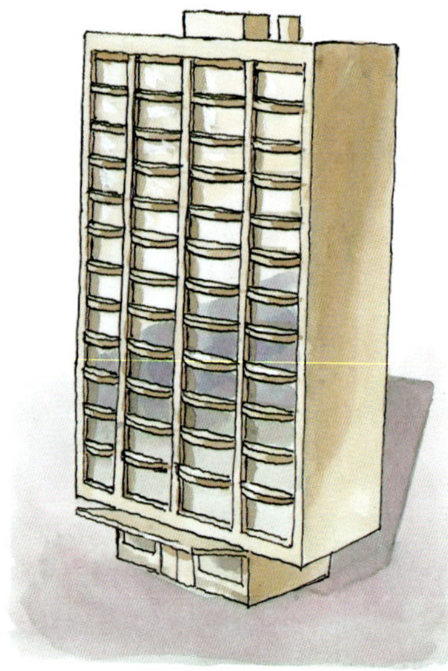

Steel bars can be set in the concrete to make it even stronger. This is called re-inforced concrete. Tall buildings are made from huge, ready-made blocks of re-inforced concrete. The blocks are made at a factory and brought to the building site by large lorries.

**ACTIVITY**

Look at the picture on this page and say how concrete is used and where you think it needs to be strongest.

## Different concrete mixes

Moulds (e.g. margarine pots) • cement • sand • small stones • water • measures •

Some children are helping to make a pond at their school. They are testing these three different concrete mixes to find the strongest.

A

B

C

ACTIVITY

Always wear rubber gloves and safety spectacles when you are handling cement.

Plan an investigation to find out which mix is strongest. Think about:

- in what way the mixes need to be strong
- how you will test their strength
- and what you will use to measure.

Talk to your teacher about your plan.

Collect the things you will need and carry out your investigation.

RECORD

Write a report for a cement factory showing what you found out.

# 4 BUILDING BRIDGES

When *engineers* design things which need to stand up to a lot of force they:

- choose strong materials
- find ways to make the materials even stronger
- use shapes which will stand up to a lot of force.

All bridges needs to be able to carry a lot of weight and very high bridges need to stay up in strong winds.

Here are four different kinds of bridges:

Suspension Bridge

Beam Bridge    Cantilever Bridge    Bowstring Girder Bridge

**ACTIVITY**

Look at each of these photographs of bridges. Use the pictures above to decide which kind of bridges they are.

Tyne Bridge

Forth Railway Bridge

Severn Bridge

Orwell Bridge

For each bridge think about the kinds of materials and shapes that have been used.

## Building bridges

Card • strong glue •
string • weights • a tray of damp sand • your own ideas

ACTIVITY
– A –

When engineers design bridges they often use models to test their ideas. Can you use models to find out where the strongest and weakest points are on the different kinds of bridges?

Make some different kinds of bridges like these:

Plan your test.
Think about how you will make your bridge stand up.
How will you make your test fair?
Try your test.

ACTIVITY
– B –

Can you plan a test to find out:
- which design is best for long bridges?
- which design is best for high bridges?

RECORD

How will you show what you find out?

# 5 GIRDERS AND BEAMS

Very tall buildings like this office block are made using a strong steel frame which is then filled in with bricks or large concrete blocks.

Older buildings like this one often had a wooden frame with a clay filling.

## Making and testing beams

Card • strong glue or sticky tape • your own ideas for testing

Most modern buildings use steel or concrete beams or *girders* to support their roofs, the walls above their window and door frames, and their upstairs rooms.
These children are testing some card beams to find out which is the strongest shape.

**ACTIVITY – A –**

Make some card beams like these.

Plan a test to find out which beam is strongest.
Talk to your teacher about your test.
How will you make sure that your test is fair?

Which of your beams do you think will be the strongest?
Why? Try your test. What do you find out?
Why might this beam be the strongest?

**ACTIVITY – B –**

Plan and carry out an investigation to find out if your beam is strongest at the ends or in the middle. Can you explain your results?

**OTHER IDEAS**

Use your strongest kind of beam to make a model climbing frame.
How will you find out how much weight it can carry?

# 6 MAKING IT STRONGER

Thin materials can be made stronger. Cardboard comes in different thicknesses. The different thicknesses can be made by:

- joining different numbers of sheets together
- using thicker paper pulp
- making *corrugated cardboard.*

These catalogue pictures show different kinds of cardboard. Can you say why different types have been used?

## ACTIVITY – A –

Look around your school. Make a list of any cardboard things you find. Make a chart like this to show:

- what you found
- what kind of cardboard was used
- why you think that kind was used.

| Thing's I Found | Kind of car board | why |
|---|---|---|
| book cover | Very thin coloured | look nice |
| box | sorong brown | hold heavy things |
| Notice | thick coloured | look nice stog strong |
| inside paper roll | very thick | strong |
| model house | thin coloured | easy to Fold look nice |
| folder | thick coloured | strong look nice |

## ACTIVITY – B –

Plan a test to find out if corrugated cardboard is stronger than the cardboard used to make cereal boxes.
Talk to your teacher about your plan before you test.

## Strengthening paper

ACTIVITY
– A –

Even a very thin material like paper can be made stronger.
Cut some strips of paper. Make each strip the same size.
Put one strip between two blocks.
How will you keep the paper on the blocks?
What weight will the paper hold?
Stick two pieces of paper together.
What will it hold now?

ACTIVITY
– B –

Can you plan a fair test to find out:

- how many sheets you need to hold 50g, 100g, and 200g weights?
- how much stronger card is than paper?

RECORD

Make a table like this to show what different numbers of sheets will hold.
Use your results to say how you would help someone to:

- make a stronger paper bag?
- make a stronger paper aeroplane?

| Number of sheets | Weight held |
| --- | --- |
| 1 | |
| 2 | |
| 3 | |
| 4 | |
| 5 | |
| 6 | |
| 7 | |
| 8 | |

OTHER IDEAS

Can a paper bridge be strong enough for someone to sit on? How will you find out?

# 7 CARRYING HEAVY LOADS

ACTIVITY

People have used many different ways to carry heavy loads. Early people carried loads in packs, on wooden frames or across their shoulders.

Try using these ways to move a heavy bag. Which way do you find easiest? Why?

## Using rollers, sledges and wheels

Things to make a buggy and a sledge • rollers • heavy objects • a forcemeter • your own ideas

ACTIVITY

People found ways of using rollers, sledges and wheels to help them move heavy loads.
Plan an investigation to find out how much force it takes to move a heavy load using these three different ways.
Carry out your investigation and show what you have found out.
Which way needed most force, and which needed least force?
Which way would you use to move a heavy load:

- upstairs?
- along a road?
- across the snow?

## Pulling loads on different surfaces

Horses were also used to move things. Pack horses carried loads on each side. The Vikings used horse-drawn carts with skis for moving on snow and ice. Strong horses were used to move heavy loads in barges along rivers.

ACTIVITY

Find out if it is easier to pull a load on water than on land.
Collect the things you need.
Carry out your investigation.
Show what you find out.

Can you use a forcemeter to find out how much easier it is to pull a load on water?

OTHER IDEAS

Use your investigations to find out the easiest ways of moving heavy loads on different surfaces.

RECORD

Write about what you did and what you found out.

# 8 MATCHING FORCES

Usually when a force works in one direction another force works in the opposite direction.

## ACTIVITY – A –

Put both hands on a wall and push. Can you feel the wall "pushing" back? The force of your push against the wall is the same as the force of the wall pushing back so nothing moves.

## ACTIVITY – B –

Choose a friend. Stand either side of a half-open door. Keep your hands away from the hinges. After a count of 3, both of you should push against the door as hard as you can. If the door doesn't move your pushing forces are equal. What does it mean if the door does move?

## ACTIVITY – C –

Look at these pictures.
Can you say:

- which ways the forces are working?
- which forces are strongest?
- and what sorts of movement will take place?

Look at these pictures and tell the story. The arrows show the different forces.

Some adults are pushing the car but the car won't move so it feels as if it is pushing back. When the car engine starts and the car moves forward nothing is pushing back so they fall over. They land on the ground with a bump which feels as if the earth is pushing back at them.

## The force of the wind

When you are walking along, the push of your body forward is greater than the push of the air against you.
A very strong wind blowing into your face slows you up and makes you have to work a lot harder to move forwards. If the force of the wind was equal to the push of your body you would stay still. What would happen if the force of the wind was stronger than your push?

### ACTIVITY

Can you make up a story like this one which shows how the strength of different forces can make things change direction? You could write it down, draw cartoons or make a tape.

# 9 CRANES AND LIFTS

When you hold a weight you can feel gravity pulling it down on your hand. If you want to lift a heavy weight the pulling up force on the weight must be greater than the pulling down force of gravity.

When people want to lift very heavy loads they use machines to help them. Cranes can lift vehicles, machines and huge pieces of buildings using pulleys.

## How much do pulleys help?

pieces of wood • 2 small wheels (meccano or lego)
hammer • nail • string • hook • weights • a forcemeter

**ACTIVITY – A –**

Use the forcemeter to find out:

1. how much force it takes to lift a weight like this?
2. how much force it takes to lift the same weight using a simple pulley?

Which way felt the easiest? Why?
Which way took most force?

**ACTIVITY**
**– B –**

Now make a pulley like this.

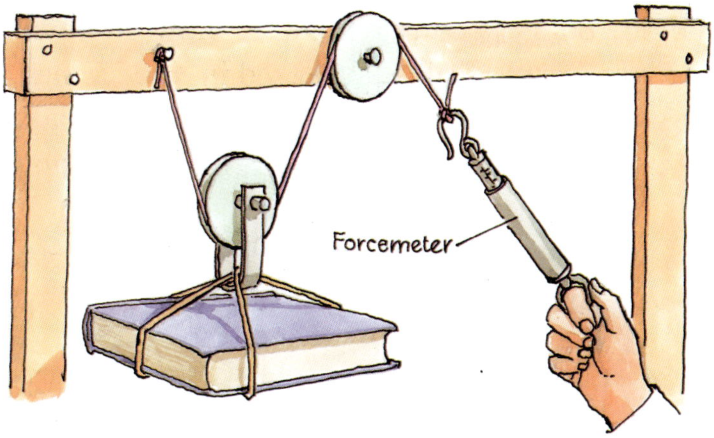


Lift the same weight again.
Which way is easiest now?
Which way took least force?

## Moving loads

These things use pulleys to move people or loads in different ways.

Cranes loading ships with heavy crates

Lifts carrying people up tall buildings

Cable cars carrying people up mountains

**ACTIVITY**

Can you make a model crane, lift or cable car?
You could use these children's models to give you ideas or use your own idea. Plan what you will do and use.
Make your model.
Test to find out how much your model can lift.

# 10 USING AIR

When you use a bicycle pump to blow up a tyre you are forcing air into the tyre. As more air is squeezed in, it becomes squashed or *compressed*, and pushes against the inside of the tyre. This is known as air pressure. What would happen if you went on forcing air into the tyre?

Compressed air can be used in lots of ways. Firefighters use bags to stop heavy vehicles falling over. The empty bag is placed under the side of the vehicle and then pumped up.

## Using air to move things

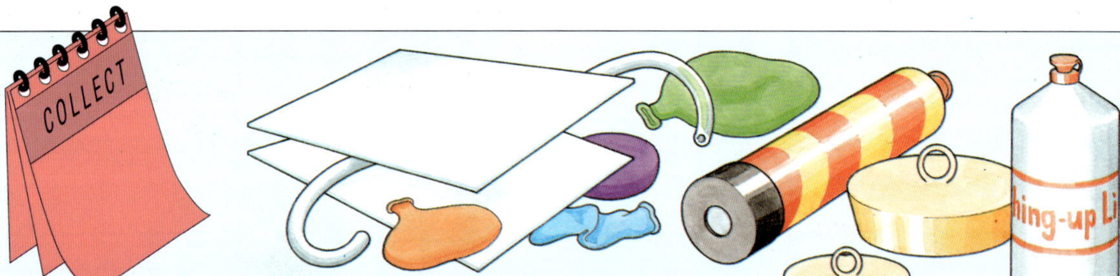

Balloons (different shapes and sizes) • tubes • pumps • card • weights • washing-up liquid bottles

**ACTIVITY – A –**

Make an air bag like this. Find out how much weight it can hold.

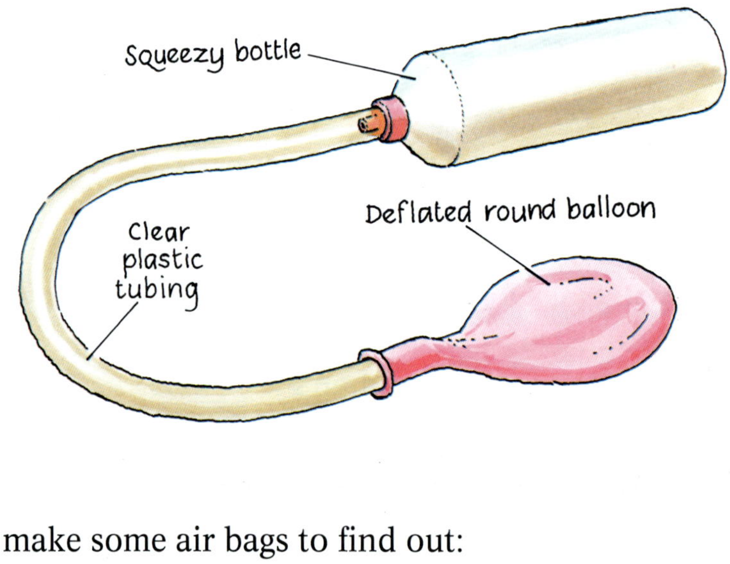


**ACTIVITY – B –**

Can you make some air bags to find out:

- ▸ if big balloons can hold more weight than small balloons?
- ▸ if round balloons can hold more weight than long balloons?
- ▸ or use your own ideas.

## RECORD

Make a record to show your results.

## ACTIVITY - C -

You make this toy work by squeezing a ball of air. The air pushes along the tube and fills a bag under the body which pushes the toy up. What do you think happens to the air when you let go of the ball?

You can make a toy using these ideas to help you.

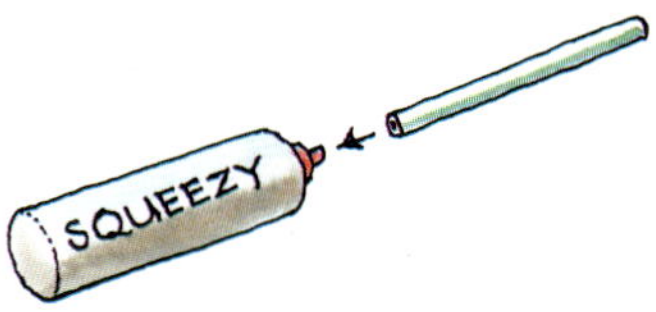


1. Attach tubing to bottle.

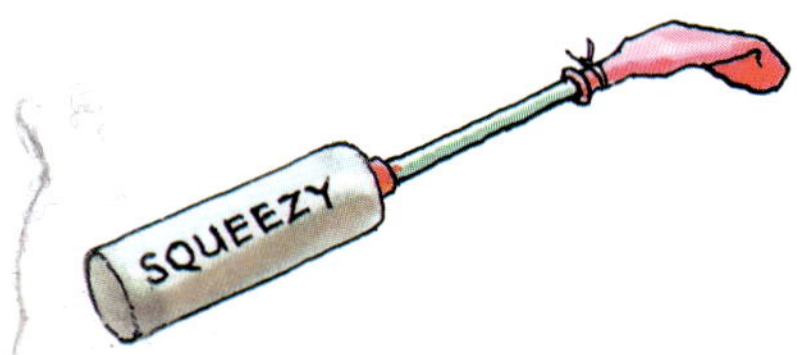


2. Pull balloon over end of tubing.

3. Attach you model to the balloon.

## OTHER IDEAS

Can you use this diagram to make a model rocket launcher?
Find an open space to try your launcher.

# 11 PUSHES AND PULLS

When you sit on a strong table, your weight is pulled down onto it by the force of gravity. The pushing down of your weight is the same as the upwards push of the table so the table stays the same.

If you sit on a thin piece of wood it will bend. Your weight is pushing down harder than the wood is pushing up. The more the wood bends the harder it pushes upwards. When the upwards push of the wood is the same as the downwards push of your weight the wood will stop bending.

What will happen here?

## Squeezing forces

This girl is squeezing the plastic bottle to make the tomato sauce come out. At first, the force of her squeezing is not as strong as the push of the bottle so the sauce stays in the bottle. When the force of her squeeze is greater than the push of the bottle the sauce will come out.

**ACTIVITY**
**– A –**

Do this activity with some friends. Everyone should stand on a line in the playground with a plastic bottle full of water. Face the same direction. On the count of 3 everyone should squeeze their bottle as hard as they can.
Whose jet of water goes the furthest distance?
Whose goes the shortest distance?
Why do you think that some jets go further than others?

Do the activity again. This time find a way to measure the length of the different jets.

**ACTIVITY**
**– B –**

Plan a fair test to find out if the length of the water jet depends on:

- the shape and size of the bottle?
- the size of the bottleneck?
- how hard you squeeze?
- or your own ideas.

**OTHER IDEAS**

Can you find out if the ball that is easiest to squeeze makes the best bouncer?

# 12 USING LIQUIDS

When you fill a bottle with water the water pushes against the sides and takes the shape of the bottle. We call this pushing force water pressure.

## Where is water pressure greatest?

A plastic bottle with a screw top • a hand drill • sticky tape • a tray • your own ideas for measuring

**ACTIVITY – A –**

Carefully make four small holes down one side of a plastic bottle. Cover the holes with tape. Fill the bottle with water and stand it on a tray. Quickly take the tape off the holes. What happens?

The greater the pressure the further the water will travel.
Where is the pressure greatest?
Why do you think this is?
What happens as the water goes down in the bottle? Why? Find out if there is a pattern of how much water is above the hole and how far the water travels.

**ACTIVITY – B –**

What happens if you do the activity again with the lid screwed on? Can you say why? How can you make the water come out all of the holes?

## Pushing liquids

COLLECT

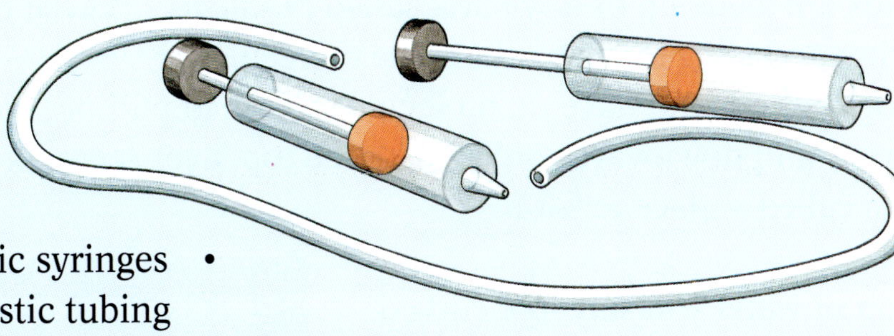

2 plastic syringes • a length of plastic tubing

Hydraulic machines use liquids to push and move different parts. Some types of cars use liquid to push the brake pads against the wheels to stop them turning.

ACTIVITY
– A –

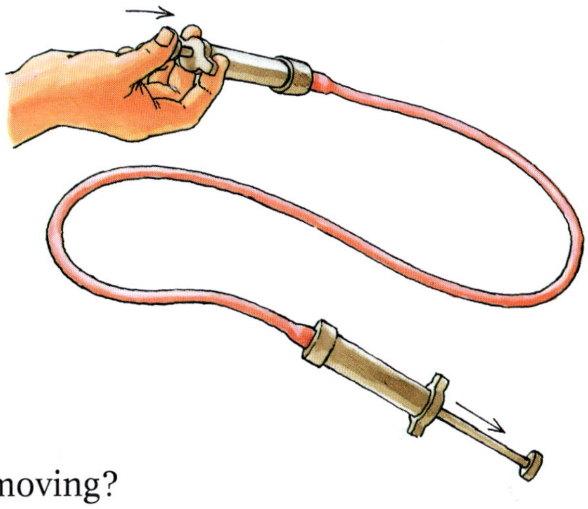

Use this diagram to make a hydraulic brake model.
Press the syringe handles in one at a time to make the model work like a car's brakes.
Can you use this idea to stop a model moving?

OTHER IDEAS

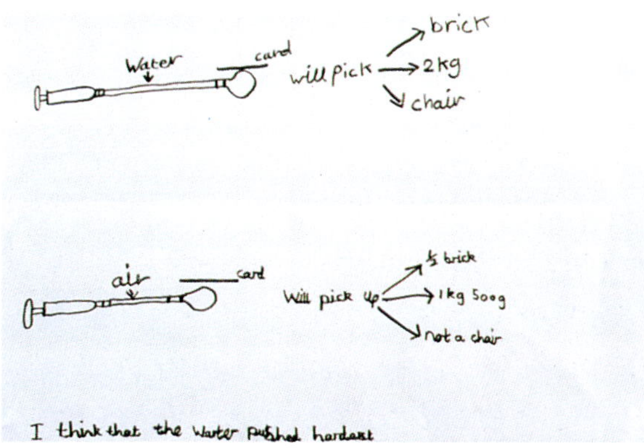


Can you plan an investigation to find out if water pressure or air pressure can push up the greatest weight?
Try your ideas.

RECORD

Write a report to show what you find out.

# 13 INVESTIGATING LIQUIDS

Liquids are made up of tiny parts called *molecules*. These parts pull together and cling to each other. The molecules at the top of the liquid have no molecules above to pull on, so the sideways and downwards pulls make the top layer seem like a skin. This is called surface tension.

A drop of water will stay in a curved shape because the surface tension pulls the water into the smallest possible shape.

## Watching surface tension

Two large bowls • pieces of drinking straws • soap washing-up liquid • cooking oil • your own ideas

ACTIVITY
– A –

Make a drop of water on a table. Now mix some soapy water and make another drop. What do you notice about the two drops?
The soap in the water separates the molecules and weakens the surface tension. The water will probably spread further.

## ACTIVITY
## – B –

Can you see how the weight of this pond-skater bends the surface of the water?
Try floating a paper clip or pin on the surface of the water.
What happens to the skin?
What happens if you add washing-up liquid?

## ACTIVITY
## – C –

Fill two bowls with water and float pieces of drinking straw on the top of each. Put some drops of washing-up liquid in the middle of one bowl.
What happens?
The soap weakens the surface tension in the middle of the bowl so the straws are pulled to the edges.

## OTHER IDEAS

Can you investigate to find out :

- if heating water affects the surface tension?
- if other kinds of liquids (e.g. milk, oil etc) have surface tension?
- or your own ideas.

**RECORD** Find a way to record your results.

# 14 REDUCING FRICTION

If you slide your feet along the floor you will feel the *friction* between your shoe and the floor.

Would there be greater friction if:

- you were on a smooth floor or a carpet?
- you wore training shoes or shoes with smooth soles?
- you were wearing roller skates or wellington boots?

This roller skater can move easily over the floor. There is very little friction between his skates and the floor. This is because the skater's wheels turn easily and the floor is smooth.
What would happen if the wheels did not turn very easily?
What would happen if he tried skating on a carpet?

This girl's bike is hard to pedal, because there is a lot of friction between the pedals and the frame. She is using oil on the pedals. The oil works to reduce the friction.

ACTIVITY

Look at these pictures and say what is reducing friction.

## How much friction?

A can of oil • a forcemeter • your own ideas

**ACTIVITY – A –**

Plan an investigation to find out how much the oil reduces friction.
You could use one of the ideas here or your own.

Plan your investigation. Collect everything you need.
Carry out your investigation.
Record your results.

**ACTIVITY – B –**

Friction can be useful. These things all use a lot of friction. Look at the pictures and say how friction is being used.

# 15 FASTER AND SLOWER

Friction helps to slow things down. This boy is cycling along a flat road. If he stops pedalling, the bike will get slower and slower until it stops. The friction between the bike tyres and the road slows it down.

If the bike was on a downhill slope the pull of gravity would make it go faster and faster until it reached the bottom. This is called *acceleration*. The pull of gravity is stronger than the friction so the bike gets faster.

## Slowing down

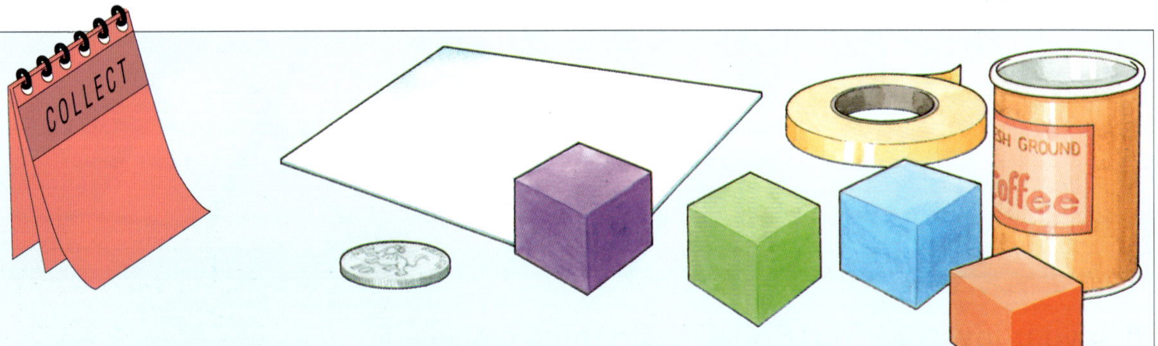


A tin • a small coin • sticky tape • things to make a slope

**ACTIVITY**
**– A –**

Tape the coin to the side of the tin. Roll the tin along a hard floor. You will hear the coin clicking against the floor. What happens as the tin slows down? What happens if you give the tin a hard push, then a gentle push?

## ACTIVITY – B –

Make a slope and roll the tin down it.
What happens now? When does the tin start to slow down?
How can you measure?
What happens if you roll it down:

- a steep slope?
- a gentle slope?

## RECORD

Make a record like this to show your results.

| Slope | Time to roll down | No of clicks |
|---|---|---|
| | 3 Secs | 4 |
| | 2 Secs | 4 |
| | 1 Secs | 4 |
| | ½ Secs | 4 |
| | ½ Secs | 4 |

## Falling and speed

When things fall they accelerate or get faster. The further things have to fall, the more time they have to get faster. The faster things fall, the harder they hit the ground.

## ACTIVITY

Do you think that a 100g ball of Plasticine dropped from 1 metre would hit the ground with more force than a 100g ball dropped from 2 metres?
Plan an investigation to find out if you are right.
Collect the things you need.
Carry out your investigation.
Make a record of your results.

## OTHER IDEAS

Hold a 100g ball of Plasticine 1 metre above a tray of damp sand and drop it. Measure the dent that it makes. Can you find a way to drop the same amount of Plasticine so that it makes a smaller dent in the sand?

# 16 ENERGY

All things which move use energy. Our energy comes from food. The amount of food we eat gives us the amount of energy that can be used. This is called potential energy.

If we put a lot of fuel in a car then it has a lot of energy that it can use. If we only put a little fuel in then there is only a small amount of energy that the car can use. When would the car have most potential energy?

**ACTIVITY**

What gives these things potential energy?

When things start to move the potential energy changes to kinetic energy. The tightly-coiled spring in this Jack-in-a-box gives the toy potential energy. When the lid is opened some of the potential energy changes to kinetic energy as the toy pops up.

## Some toys have potential energy

Card pieces • strong glue • your own ideas

**ACTIVITY – A –**

1. Make a box like this.

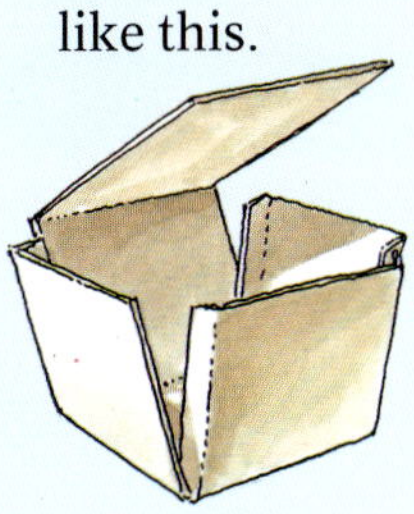

2. Fold a card spring.

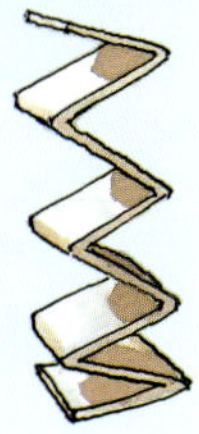

3. Stick your card spring in your box and decorate.

**ACTIVITY – B –**

Look at these toys. Say what gives each one potential energy.

How do they move when the potential energy changes to kinetic energy?

# 17 FUELS

Most homes and schools use energy from fuels like oil, gas, wood, coal or electricity. Some homes like this one are heated by solar heating which uses energy from the sun.

## Solar heating

2 pieces of plastic tubing • thermometer • Plasticine • black plastic • newspaper

ACTIVITY

Something to try on a sunny day.
Put Plasticine over one end of the tubes and fill them with cold water.
Find the temperature of the water.
Put Plasticine over the other end of the tubes. Lay both tubes in a sunny place but put one tube on newspaper and cover it with black plastic.
Take the temperature of the water in the tubes every hour.
Keep a chart to show the times and the temperatures. What do you notice?
Why might the water temperature in the two tubes be different?
Leave the tubes out overnight. Take the temperature again in the morning.
What do you notice now?

## A school heating survey

Most fuels are expensive to use and we shall eventually run out of fuels like coal, oil and gas so people look for ways of saving fuel. A heating survey can help to find out where buildings lose most heat.

**ACTIVITY – A –**

Collect some thermometers and use them to find out where the warmest and coldest places are in your school. You could start in your classroom. Put your thermometers in different places like:

window sills

near radiators

by doors

on top of cupboards

**RECORD**

Carefully note down the temperatures in the different places.
Draw a chart or a plan like this one to show your results.

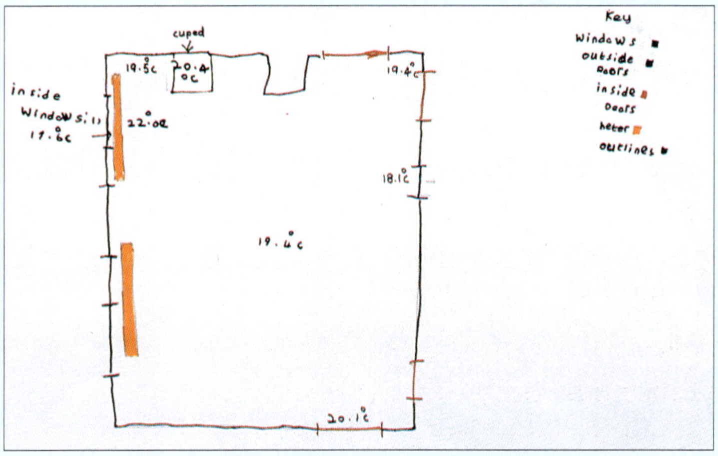


**ACTIVITY – B –**

Use your results to say where you think your school might lose most heat. Use your thermometers to find out if you are right. Can you use what you find out to help your school to save heat and fuel?

# 18 FLOWING ELECTRICITY

Electricity can be very dangerous.
If something goes wrong with an electrical circuit, the electricity finds the quickest way to the ground. If someone is touching the circuit the electricity will go through them and give them a shock.

Never touch someone who is having an electric shock because the electricity will go through you and give you a shock. First the power should be turned off. Then something which will not *conduct* electricity should be used to move the person. What is being used here? Why?

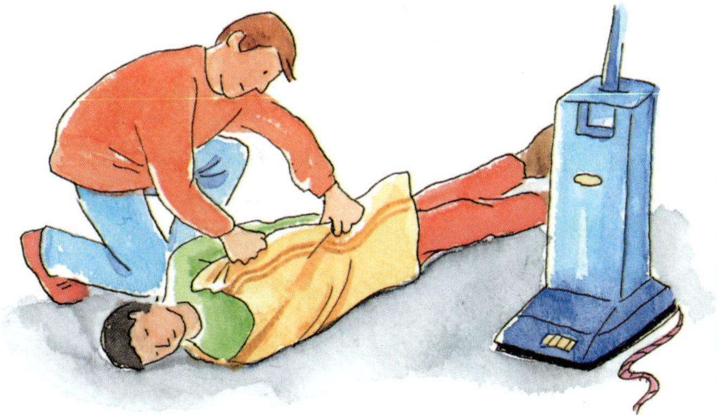

ACTIVITY

We can safely use batteries and bulbs to investigate things which will or will not conduct electricity.
Never play with mains electricity.

Plan and carry out an investigation using batteries and bulbs to show which things would be safe to use to move someone who is having an electric shock. Talk to your teacher about your plan. Collect the things you need and carry out your investigation.

RECORD

Show your results in a way that will prove to someone else that these things are safe. Show what you used and why.

## Making a resistor

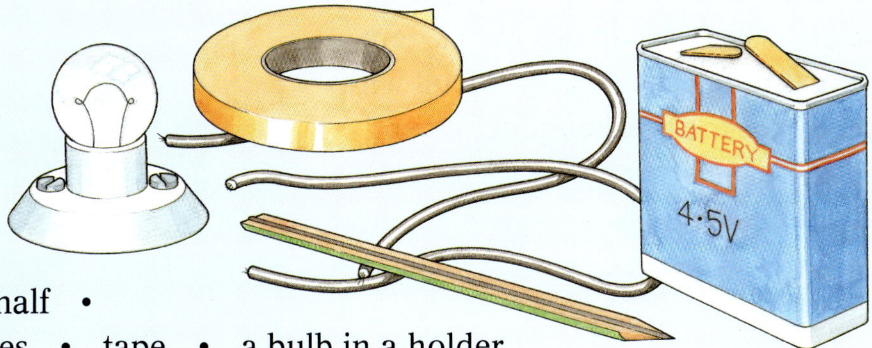


A pencil split in half • a battery • wires • tape • a bulb in a holder

Good conductors are things which let the electricity move through them easily. Sometimes the electric current meets things which cut it down or stop it from flowing around a circuit. Insulators stop the current moving and resistors slow it down.

### ACTIVITY

Make an open circuit.

Tape the end of one of the wires to the pencil so that it is touching the graphite. Hold the other wire on the graphite near to the first wire. Move the wire until the bulb lights up.
Now slowly move the wire to the other end of the graphite watching the bulb. What happens? The graphite is acting like a resistor.

### OTHER IDEAS

Dimmer switches are often used in bedrooms. The lights can be turned down so they are not too bright. Can you make a model which uses a dimmer switch?

# 19 ELECTRICAL ENERGY

Good conductors are materials, like metals, which let an electric current move through them easily. Metal wires and cables are good conductors and this is how electricity comes to our homes and schools.

In our homes we have different circuits which carry the electricity to different places. The circuits all start at a control box where the electricity comes into the house. This is what the inside of a control box looks like.

Most homes have three kinds of circuits:

- a lighting circuit which travels through a chain of lights
- a ring circuit which goes around the house joining all the sockets
- and single circuits which go to things like cookers, which use a lot of power.

ACTIVITY

Find the different circuits on this diagram.

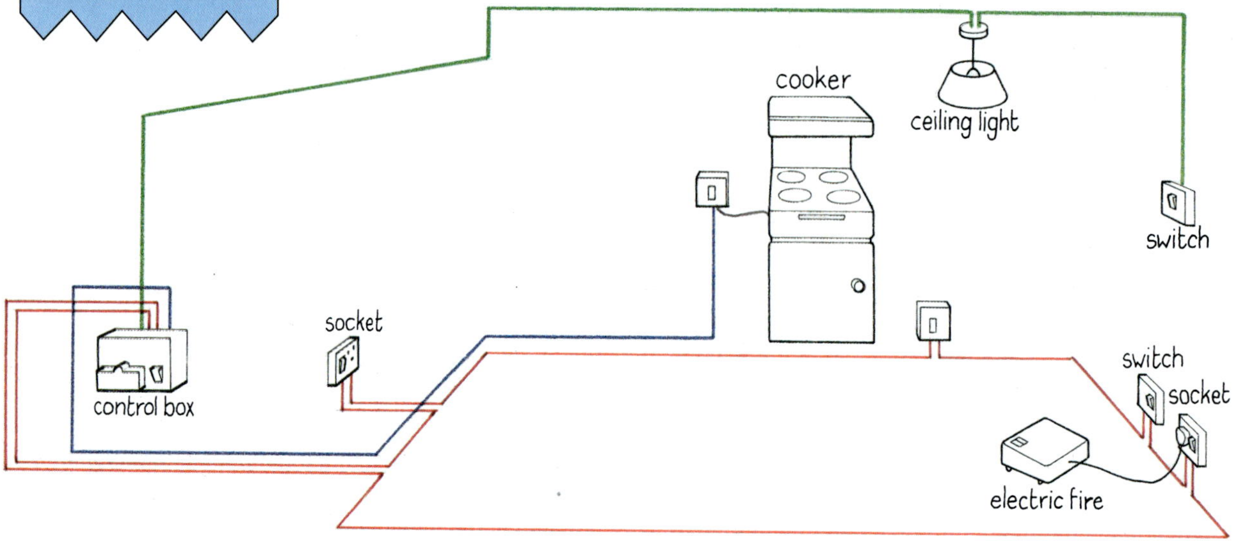

# Making a model room with a lighting circuit

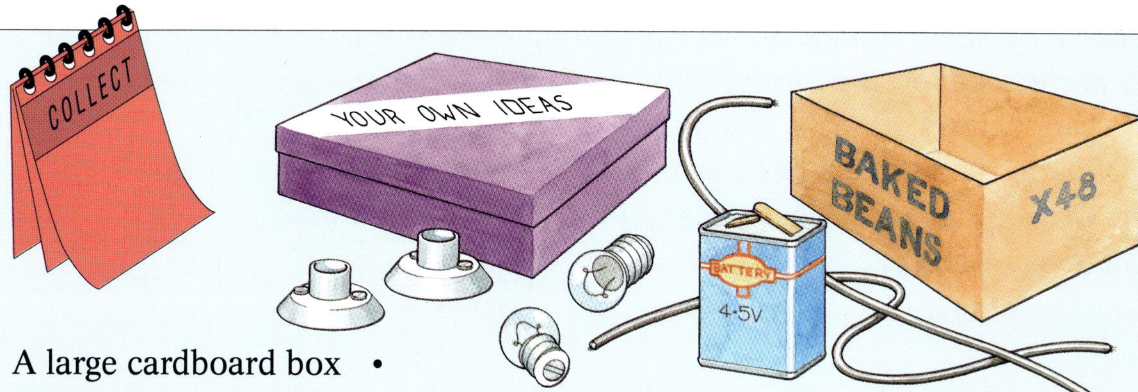


A large cardboard box • light bulbs and holders • wires • batteries • your own ideas

## ACTIVITY – A –

We can safely use batteries and bulbs to investigate circuits. Never play with mains electricity.

Make a model room like this one with two or more lights. Use the battery as the control box. Can you make it so that one light stays on if the other is broken? Can you add more lights to your lighting chain?

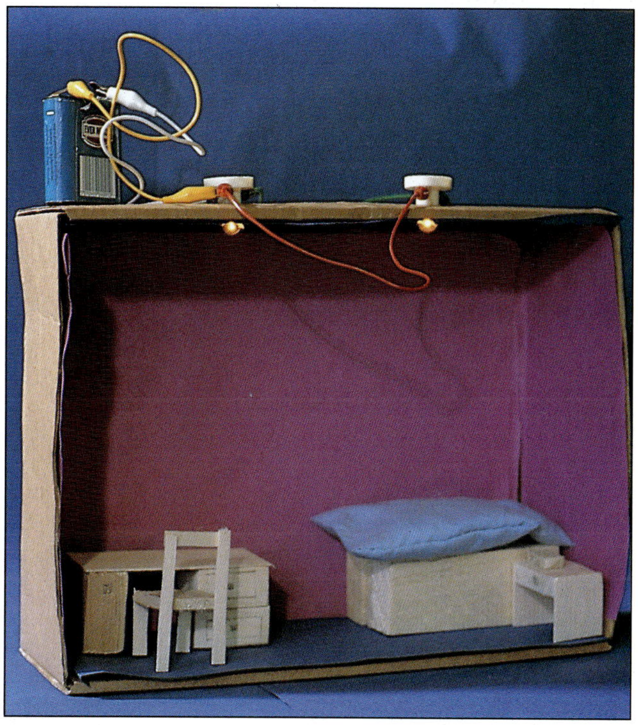

## ACTIVITY – B –

Draw a plan of your model room using these symbols for:

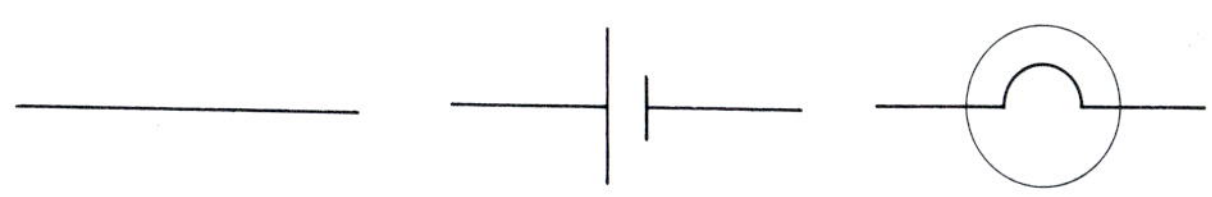

wires batteries bulbs.

## OTHER IDEAS

Can you add a switch to your room? Use this symbol to put it on your plan.

# 20 CONTROLLING ENERGY

Electricity in our homes is controlled in different ways:

- switches allow the current through when we want to use it, and we can switch it off when we don't
- thermostats switch the current off when the temperature gets high enough, and on again if it begins to cool down – like an iron
- transformers change *voltages* up and down.

Some machines like these use switches to control what happens.

These machines use controls called logic gates.
There are three main kinds of logic gates:

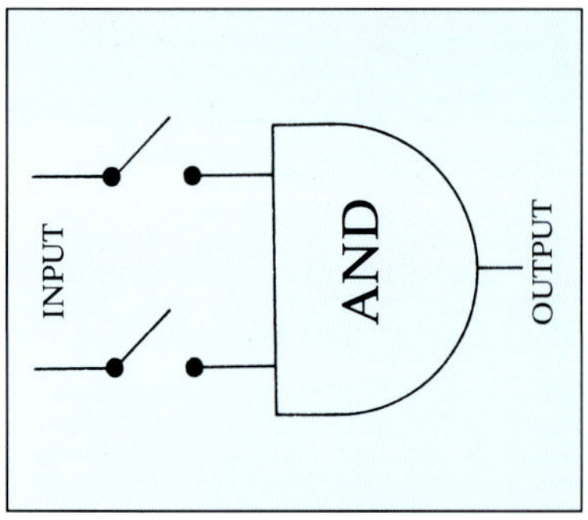


AND gates - where both of the switches have to be closed before the machine will work.

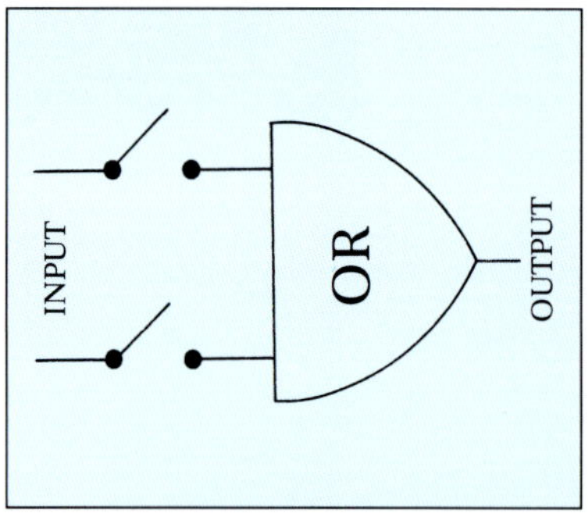


OR gates - where closing either switch will work the machine.

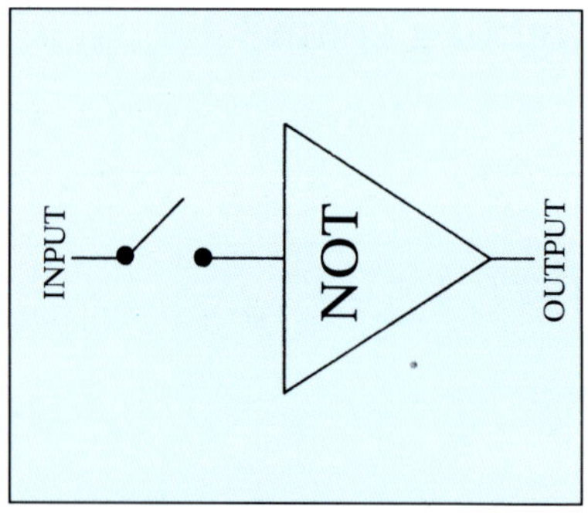


NOT gates - where if the switch is closed the machine will not work and if the switch is open the machine will work.

## ACTIVITY – A –

You can see how these different logic gates work by making some circuits with switches like these:

AND gate

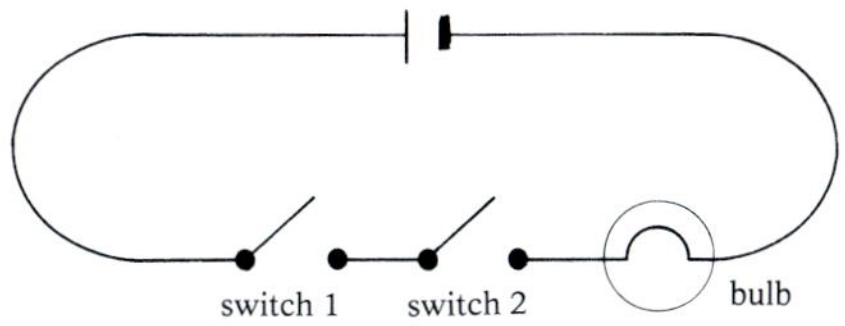


The bulb lights up if both switches 1 AND 2 are closed

OR gate

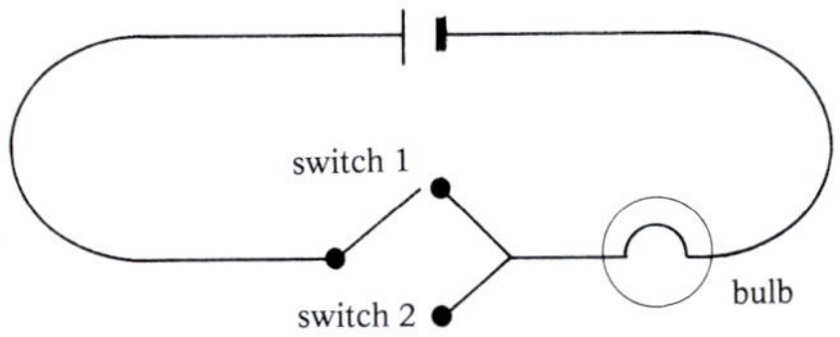


The bulb lights up if either switch 1 OR switch 2 is closed

NOT gate

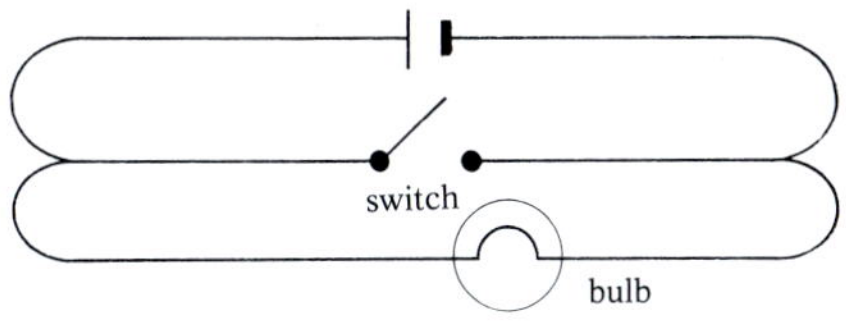


The bulb lights up if the switch is NOT closed

## ACTIVITY – B –

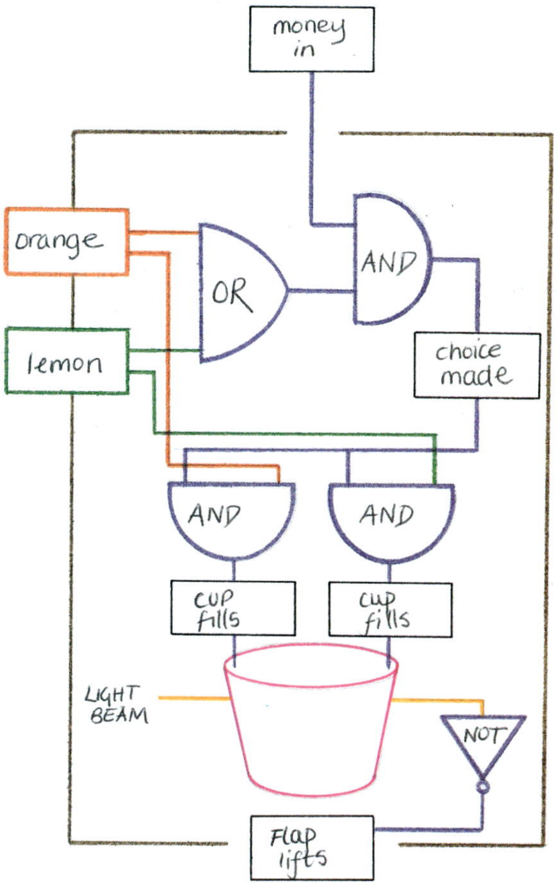


This drinks machine was invented by some children.

The top AND gate says that there must be money in and a choice made before a drink can be given.

The OR gate gives a choice of lemonade or orange juice.

The NOT gate tells the machine that the cup is full when the light beam cannot pass through it.

Do you think this machine would work? Can you think of ways to improve it?

# Glossary

**Acceleration**
Acceleration is the rate at which the speed of something is increasing.

**Cement**
Cement is a fine grey powder made from limestone and clay. It is mixed with sand and water. It hardens when it is dry.

**Compressed**
When something is compressed it is squeezed or shortened so that it takes up less space.

**Conduct**
If something conducts electricity, it allows electricity to pass through it. Most metals conduct electricity.

**Corrugated**
If something is corrugated, it is ridged or grooved.

**Engineers**
An engineer is someone who designs and builds machinery, buildings, roads and bridges.

**Fired**
When a brick is fired, it is put into a kiln to bake and harden.

**Friction**
Friction happens when two surfaces rub against each other.

**Girder**
A girder is a strong metal or concrete beam which is used in the framework of a building or bridge.

**Molecule**
A molecule is a small collection of atoms. An atom is the smallest part of anything. Everything is made from atoms.

**Voltage**
The voltage of an electric current is its force measured in volts.

# Index